KARATE

by Thomas Buckley

Content Adviser: Philip S. Porter, Founder,
United States Martial Arts Association,
Citrus Heights, California

Published in the United States of America by The Child's World®
PO Box 326 • Chanhassen, MN 55317-0326 • 800-599-READ • www.childsworld.com

ACKNOWLEDGMENTS

The Child's World®: Mary Berendes, Publishing Director

Editorial Directions, Inc.: E. Russell Primm, Editorial Director; Halley Gatenby, Line Editor;
Susan Hindman, Copyeditor; Elizabeth K. Martin and Katie Marsico, Assistant Editors;
Matthew Messbarger, Editorial Assistant; Kerry Reid, Fact Checker; Tim Griffin/IndexServ,
Indexer; James Buckley Jr., Photo Researcher and Photo Selector

The Design Lab: Kathleen Petelinsek, Design and Page Production

PHOTOS

Cover: George Shelley/Corbis
TRBfoto/Photodisc, 1
AP/Wide World: 10, 15, 16
Asian Art & Archaeology/Corbis: 6
Bridgeman Art Library: 7
Bruce Burkhardt/Corbis: 26, 27
Burstein Collection/Corbis: 8
Corbis: 20, 28
David Katzenstein/Corbis: 22
Getty Images: 13, 17, 19, 25
North Wind Pictures: 4, 9
Tom Stewart/Corbis: 5
Wally McNamee/Corbis: 23

REGISTRATION

LIBRARY OF CONGRESS CATALOGING-IN-PUBLICATION DATA

Buckley, Thomas J.
  Karate / by Thomas Buckley.
    p. cm. — (Kids' guides)
Includes bibliographical references and index.
  ISBN 1-56766-751-1 (lib. bdg. : alk. paper)
  1. Karate—Juvenile literature. [1. Karate.] I. Title. II. Series.
GV1114.3.B83 2004
796.815'3—dc22   2003018079

CONTENTS

4 introduction
THE PEASANT'S ART

6 chapter one
A MONK GIVES BIRTH TO A FIGHTING ART

12 chapter two
KARATE TRAINING METHODS

17 chapter three
THE KARATE ARSENAL

22 chapter four
THE WAY OF THE EMPTY HAND

26 chapter five
MASTERING YOURSELF . . . AND OTHER WEAPONS

29 glossary

30 timeline

31 find out more

32 index

THE PEASANT'S ART

YOU HAVE PROBABLY SEEN KARATE MOVES

in movies, on television, and in video games. Shattering punches mix with high-flying kicks that are stopped by sweeping blocks. The karate fighters yell out a dramatic *"ki-ai!"*

Karate is a fighting style, or **martial art,** that teaches a system of hand strikes, kicks, and blocks. Fighting for self-defense and physical fitness are an important part of karate. More important, though, karate stresses mental toughness, compassion, spiritual well-being, and, especially, respect.

Karate developed on the Japanese island of Okinawa.

Warriors in ancient Japan were known as samurai.

4

Young people of all ages and skill levels can take part in karate classes.

In ancient times, the emperor of Japan's **samurai** conquered many of Japan's neighbors, including Okinawa. The peasants of Okinawa were forbidden by their samurai rulers to carry weapons of any kind. To defend themselves, they developed a bare-handed fighting style. That style evolved over the years to become karate.

Today, karate is taught all over the world. Very likely, there is a school in your neighborhood. Learning karate will not only improve your physical health, it can also help you do your best in every part of your life. If you train hard, study, and work, you can gain lessons of self-improvement from karate.

The cool, high-flying kicks are just a bonus.

CHAPTER ONE

A MONK GIVES BIRTH TO A FIGHTING ART

SINCE HUMANKIND'S EARLIEST DAYS,

people have needed to protect themselves. Sometimes they have

needed protection from hostile animals, and sometimes from

one another. So people of different cultures developed systems

or styles of fighting, called martial arts.

The founder of karate was not, as you might expect, a

mighty conqueror or a fierce general. He was not a mythical

creature either, although there were early legends of creatures

This painting
shows a man
battling with a
"tengu," or ancient
demon.

This statue is of Buddhist monk and martial arts pioneer Bodhidharma.

called the Tengu who taught mortals to fight. Many early teachers of martial arts claimed to have been trained by the Tengu, as a way of inspiring fear and awe in their students.

Rather, karate can trace its beginning to the workings of a wandering monk from India. Nearly 1,500 years ago, a **Zen Buddhist** monk named Bodhidharma traveled to China from India. (In Okinawa and other parts of Japan, he is known as Daruma.) His religion was based on the teachings of Zen. This is a philosophy (a system of knowledge or belief) that teaches each individual to search the self for deeper meaning. In Bodhidharma's

Lao Tzu, the founder of Taoism, is depicted riding a mule in this statue.

Shaolin Monastery, he used his Zen philosophy to develop exercises to strengthen the mind, body, and spirit. This was an early form of martial art that eventually developed into karate.

When he arrived in China, Bodhidharma's teaching combined with Chinese religions of the time. His work began to take on elements of their teachings as well. The major Chinese religions of that time were Taoism and Confucianism. Taoism

The teachings of Chinese philosopher Confucius affected the development of karate and other martial arts.

taught compassion, spiritual harmony, and balance. Confucianism's teachings included self-discipline and respect for authority. These values became important parts of the philosophy of karate.

After spreading through China, the monk's teachings also spread to neighboring lands, including Okinawa. There, Daruma's teachings found ready and willing students. The Okinawans realized that the techniques used in Daruma's exercises could also serve as a means of defense, since they couldn't carry weapons under samurai law. Modern karate developed in the cities of Okinawa, with each city developing its own distinctive style. It eventually spread beyond Okinawa, gaining the popularity it enjoys today. The spread of this martial art is largely due to the efforts of a karate master named Gichin Funakoshi. He is considered to be the father of modern karate.

In 1922, Funakoshi gave a public demonstration of karate

The Pacific island of Okinawa, where these students are practicing, remains a hotbed of karate. In 2003, an international tournament was held there with more than 4,600 athletes taking part.

at the request of the Ministry of Education in Japan. It was a huge success. With his punishing strikes, devastating kicks, and powerful blocks, Funakoshi impressed his audience with the power and potential of karate. His performance captured the attention of Crown Prince Hirohito, who later became the emperor of Japan. Hirohito's interest encouraged the spread of karate in Japan.

Funakoshi's students eventually became the most important and influential teachers of karate. Under their instruction, karate became so popular in Japan that it was eventually taught in the public schools.

Using the exercise techniques developed by a Zen Buddhist monk, karate started as a way for Okinawan peasants to defend themselves from their samurai overlords. Since then, it has become an important part of Japanese culture and of popular cultures all over the world.

WHAT *KARATE* MEANS

On Okinawa, karate was first called *te*, the Japanese word meaning "hand." Later, the art came to be known as *kara-te*, or "Chinese hand." The Chinese written character for kara could also mean "empty." So when Master Funakoshi began using the term *karate-do*, the meaning became what it is today: "the way of the empty hand."

KARATE TRAINING METHODS

KARATE IS MORE THAN JUST A WAY

to fight. However, its basic training methods do involve learning a powerful fighting method. Advanced karate students sometimes train with weapons, but for the most part, *you* are the weapon. Karate trains you to focus as much of your body's power as possible into each blow or kick. All of this power is delivered at the point of impact.

Karate's training methods are designed to help you reach this goal. For example, a huge weight lifter might be physically fit and very strong. Without knowledge of karate, though, he might not hit with the same impact as even a young karate student. The type of strength needed to lift weights is different from the strength needed to deliver a punch with impact.

To develop this kind of strength, karate students learn proper form and technique. Then they practice that form and technique over and over. Training tools are used, such as punching bags, foam-rubber shields, or hard punching boards known as *makiwara*. They are used to teach the student how to deliver the technique properly.

Before the first punch can be thrown, though, the **karateka** (person who practices karate) must learn the basics: how to stand, move, and breathe. Learning to stand properly involves practicing the stances taught in each school. A stance is a particular pose the student assumes before doing karate techniques. Stances are taught to help students with balance and to provide a strong foundation for any attack.

One commonly taught stance is the horse. In this stance, the student stands with feet just wider than shoulder-distance apart. The knees are bent, and the elbows are back with fists at hip level. In another stance, the forward stance, the student stands with the back straight and shoulders squared. One leg is bent in front, and the other is extended straight behind. Advanced students work with and learn many other stances. All of karate's stances are designed to improve

This punch comes straight out of the well-known horse stance.

the student's balance. This way, both attacks and defensive moves will be effective.

Balance is always important in karate. Any attack launched without proper balance would not be effective. The student would be unable to put any weight behind the attack. More important, a technique is not effective if you lose your balance and fall down whenever you try it!

However, perfect balance alone will not always help a karateka. The student must avoid becoming so rooted in place that an effective move cannot be launched. Movement is vital to karate. For that reason, students are taught to move smoothly between stances as they attack or defend.

Modified stances, known as fighting stances, are also taught. These stances provide much of the balance of traditional stances. They also allow for freedom of movement. In a fighting stance, the karateka tries to stay on the balls of the feet, with one foot in front of the other. This allows the student to move freely and maintain balance.

The other important part of movement is learning to put as much of the force of your body behind a blow as possible. To do this, karate students are taught to rotate their hips and shoulders into a punch. When this is done correctly, the force comes from the whole body, not just from the fist. This is the

Karate punches involve the power of the whole body, not just the arm and hand.

reason why even a small karate master can hit harder than the

biggest weight lifter. As they say in karate schools, size isn't

everything.

It might sound strange to say, but karate students need to know how to breathe properly. We have been breathing our whole lives and would not seem to need any instruction. To perform karate moves correctly, though, proper breathing is very important. Students are trained to **exhale** when performing a punch, a kick, or a block. Exhaling helps to assure that as much of the body's energy as possible is focused into the karate technique.

Breathing is part of the reason for the yell *ki-ai!* You may have heard karate practitioners yell out loudly when performing a move. This yell is called a *ki-ai*, which means "power concentration." It helps a karate student exhale forcefully when a technique is performed. Sometimes it can scare the pants off your opponent, too!

The "ki-ai!" cry helps the karate student focus his or her energy and breathing.

THE KARATE ARSENAL

KARATE LETS A STUDENT BECOME THE

weapon if a fight is absolutely necessary—for self-defense or to defend someone else. The way a body can become a weapon is by learning the moves, or techniques, of karate. These include blows with the hand (called *tsuki*), kicks with the foot *(keri)*, and blocks *(uke)*. These techniques are learned and practiced in two ways: **kata** and **kumite.**

Kumite practice help students develop and perfect their moves.

Kata is a carefully arranged sequence of blocks, kicks, and punches. These techniques are usually performed against an imaginary opponent. Students also perform kata with a partner, reacting to the techniques in the proper sequence. This is done slowly, especially with beginners, and with no actual contact.

Kumite, or sparring, involves actual fighting with an opponent, with or without contact. For training purposes, pads, headgear, and other safety equipment are worn. Contact is limited to certain areas of the body, especially for beginning and intermediate students. The idea is never to hurt your classmate or training partner. Instead, the goal of kumite is to get a better idea of what actual combat is like. You can also use your techniques at full speed.

There are many types of hand techniques available in karate's **arsenal.** Punches can be thrown quickly with the leading hand. If the rear hand in a fighting stance delivers a punch, it can be more powerful, because the hips and shoulder can be turned more. Strikes with the hand can also be made, using the palm or the side of the fist. The fingertips or the blade of the hand can also be used.

Advanced karate students learn dozens of hand techniques for different situations. For example, a strike with the

fingertips might be effective if the target is small. A hammer blow with the side of the fist is more powerful, but difficult to deliver to a small target.

When one hand is striking, the other hand is called the safety hand. This hand is used to block off the area of the body that is made vulnerable by the attack. For example, a student throwing a straight right punch will use the left hand to block the face. If a left backfist is used, the student will block off the rib area under the extended arm.

There are also many types of kicks available to a karate master. The most common are the front snap kick and the back kick. The front snap kick whips the leg straight out, quickly. Its quickness is its best advantage. The back kick lifts the leg up and shoots it straight back, like the kick of a horse or mule. It is effective for dealing with attackers coming from behind.

This side kick shows how the kicker keeps his balance on one foot while kicking out with the other.

Balance is especially important when executing kicks. When you are kicking, you will need to stand on one foot, which naturally makes balance more difficult. Balance becomes increasingly more difficult as you learn more advanced kicks, including spinning or roundhouse kicks. Because of that, advanced students must practice their kicks over and over. They must learn to deliver these techniques with power, but without falling. Nothing ruins a beautiful spinning hook kick more than falling on your behind when you finish it!

Blocks are another important part of a karateka's knowledge. The basic blocks taught in karate are inward, outward, upward, and downward. Different blocks are used depending on where the attack is coming from. The block is generally made with the forearm. As students advance, they learn to turn a block into a grab or throw. Evasive moves—ways to avoid an opponent's attack—are also taught.

Because karate is an aggressive fighting style, though, it is important to remember that the best defense is attack. Blocks are important, but an opponent cannot strike you while he or she is being punched or kicked effectively. Quick attack, in sparring or in a fight, is often the best way for a karateka to keep from getting hit.

CHAPTER FOUR

THE WAY OF THE EMPTY HAND

AS WE LEARNED EARLIER, KARATE IS

more than just a style of fighting. "The way of the empty hand" also means a way to live in spiritual and mental harmony. Karate requires that students have compassion for others. They should also have self-discipline; an appreciation for hard work; and respect for their teachers, parents, and country. Master Funakoshi described it this way:

Martial arts can help train your mind to focus and relax, as well as help your body develop.

True Karate-do is this: that in daily life one's mind and body be trained and developed in a spirit of humility, and that in critical times, one be devoted utterly to the cause of justice.

This way of living is developed in the student through karate training. Proper training will help a student in all parts of life.

A student's body is made stronger and healthier through hard exercise. This includes holding the proper stances. It also means perfecting karate techniques through constant practice and repetition. After an hour of kicks, strikes, and blocks, you'll discover that karate is a great workout!

This physical exercise helps a student's mental health, too. The self-discipline will help students excel in schoolwork

Karate class is a great way to spend time with friends, too!

or in anything else they do. In fact, many karate masters insist that their students get good grades in school in order to advance in rank as karateka. Any respectable karate teacher will also insist that students stay away from drugs, smoking, and other unhealthy influences.

Another benefit karate can provide is self-confidence. The skills learned in kata and kumite give students the knowledge they can use to protect themselves. Karate is intended for self-defense. Students are taught to always avoid a fight, if possible. But the self-confidence gained from karate extends into every area of the karateka's life.

Finally, tournaments and competitions teach karate students respect and good sportsmanship. Competitors are required by the rules of the sport to show respect for each other and for the judges. They must bow before and after each match and always show good sportsmanship. These values can also be helpful in other areas of life, outside of the karate studio.

For this reason, all of karate's training methods are designed to develop more than just the ability to fight. For example, kata and stances help develop balance, attention to detail, and self-discipline. Performing kata and kumite teach self-control and mutual respect. The strategic planning needed in a sparring match helps to develop the intellect.

Teachers work carefully with students to show them the proper way to perform karate.

All of this combines to make karate great exercise and a powerful self-defense system. It also teaches a way of living that will help students succeed at whatever they wish to do.

CHAPTER FIVE

MASTERING YOURSELF . . . AND OTHER WEAPONS

AFTER YEARS OF TRAINING, KARATE

masters know dozens of ways to use their art in self-defense.
Many study other martial arts as well. Their bodies truly
become the only weapon they need.

Advanced students of karate can learn to use the traditional weapons of karate as well. Remember that the Okinawan
peasants were forbidden to carry weapons. Some students of
karate history believe that the peasants did have some weapons,

Some advanced
students can learn
to use the staff,
called a "bo."

anyway. These were prob-
ably homemade, perhaps out of
farming tools.

The *bo* is a staff, or pole, a
little more than 6 feet (2 meters)
long. The peasants probably had
many such poles, such as walking
sticks and rake handles. The bo is
a long, straight staff that can be
used to strike or to block. In some
schools, even beginning or intermediate students are taught kata
using the bo.

Another weapon is the
nunchaku, two shorter sticks
connected by a chain or a rope.
This weapon may have developed
from a farm tool called a rice
flail. In the hands of a master,
the nunchaku can be whirled
around the body and spun from hand to hand very dramatically.

The nunchaku is modeled after a flail, a kind of farm instrument.

Other weapons come in pairs, with one used in each hand.
Tonfa are short clubs with a handle on the side. They look like

the nightsticks police sometimes carry. *Sai* are like big steel forks. They have a long prong on each side, to be used in catching and blocking other weapons. *Kama* are short sticks with **sickle blades** at the ends.

Practice with these weapons strengthens the teachings of self-discipline and control that lie at karate's heart. As with all of a karateka's training, this practice helps develop self-confidence, mental and physical health, and respect. Learning to fight is one thing, but karate will give you much more.

Respect for opponents and each other is an important part of all martial arts practice.

GLOSSARY

arsenal—a place where weapons are kept; also, a person's collection of weapons or powers

exhale—to breathe out

flail—a farm tool made of two long sticks connected at one end with rope or a chain

karateka—a person who practices karate

kata—a technique of practicing karate moves without contact; the term also refers to a series of moves practiced in a planned sequence

kumite—a technique of practicing karate moves with and without contact against an opponent

martial art—a fighting sport or skill, especially one developed in Asian lands

samurai—a warrior class who fought for the emperor of Japan

sickle blades—short, curved blades usually attached to wooden handles, used on farms for cutting crops

Zen Buddhist—a follower of the form of the Buddhist religion originally practiced in Japan and now practiced worldwide

TIMELINE

1609   Okinawa is captured by Japan; samurai rulers forbid citizens from having weapons.

1922   Okinawan master Gichin Funakoshi demonstrates karate techniques for Japan's Ministry of Education.

1938   Shotokan Karate School is founded by Gichin Funakoshi.

1956   Tsutomu Ohshima opens the first karate schools in the United States.

1959   Black belts are first awarded to American students.

1970   The first World Karate Championships are held in Toyko, Japan.

1984   The motion picture *The Karate Kid* is released, increasing interest in young Americans in karate and other martial arts.

FIND OUT MORE

Books

Brightfield, Richard. *Master of Karate.* Milwaukee: Gareth Stevens, 1995.

Dunphy, Michael J. *The Kids' Karate Book.* New York: Workman, 1999.

Jensen, Julie. *Beginning Karate.* Minneapolis: Lerner, 1998.

Queen, J. Allen. *Learn Karate.* New York: Sterling, 1998.

Simmons, Alex. *Karate Kids Want to Win! Number One Series.* Mahwah, N.J.: Troll Communications, 2002.

On the Web

Visit our home page for lots of links about karate:
http://www.childsworld.com/links.html

NOTE TO PARENTS, TEACHERS, AND LIBRARIANS: We routinely check our Web links to make sure they're safe, active sites—so encourage your readers to check them out!

INDEX

back kick, 20
balance, 13, 14, 21, 24
blocks (uke), 16, 17, 19, 21
bo (staff), 27
Bodhidharma, 7–8, 9
breathing, 16

China, 8, 9
Confucianism, 8, 9

Daruma, 7, 9–10
downward blocks, 21

exercise, 23
exhaling, 16

fighting stance, 14, 18
form, 12
forward stance, 13
front snap kick, 20
Funakoshi, Gichin, 10–11, 22

hammer blow, 19
hand strikes (tsuki), 12, 13,
    14–15, 16, 17, 18–19
Hirohito, emperor of Japan,
    11

horse stance, 13

inward blocks, 21

Japan, 5

kama (weapon), 28
kata techniques, 17–18, 24
keri (kicks), 16, 17, 20–21
ki-ai yell, 16
kicks (keri), 16, 17, 20–21
kumite (sparring), 17, 18, 24

makiwara (punching boards),
    12
martial arts, 4, 6
Ministry of Education (Japan),
    11

nunchaku (weapon), 27

Okinawa, 4–5, 9–10, 11, 26
outward blocks, 21

punches. See hand strikes.
punching boards (makiwara),
    12

rice flail, 27
roundhouse kicks, 21

safety hand, 19
sai (weapon), 28
self-confidence, 24
self-discipline, 22, 23–24
Shaolin Monastery, 7–8
sparring (kumite), 17, 18, 24
spirituality, 22–23
sportsmanship, 24
stance, 12–14, 18, 23, 24

Taoism, 8–9
technique, 12, 17, 18
Tengu (mythical creature), 7
tonfa (weapon), 27–28
training tools, 12
tsuki (hand strikes), 12, 13,
    14–15, 16, 17, 18–19

uke (blocks), 16, 17, 19, 21
upward blocks, 21

weapons, 12, 26–28

Zen Buddhism, 7, 8

ABOUT THE AUTHOR

Thomas Buckley is an attorney and writer in Raleigh, North Carolina, who has won several screenwriting awards. In 1997, he was honored to earn a student black belt in Kenpo Karate from Grandmaster Rick Allemany in San Francisco. He has also participated in seminar training in the arts of jujitsu, *arnis, escrima, wing chun,* and kung fu Sansoo. His one-year-old son already has a pretty good front kick and an impressive *ki-ai,* and his five-year-old daughter is formidable!